Elephants for Kids

by Anthony D. Fredericks
illustrated by John F. McGee

NORTHWORD PRESS
Minnetonka, Minnesota

WILDLIFE *for Kids* **SERIES** ™

DEDICATION
For Aunt Jean

Photography 1998: Mark J. Thomas/Dembinsky Photo Associates: cover, 16-17; Joe McDonald/Tom Stack & Associates: 3, 23, 44-45; Art Wolfe: 4-5, 14, 36-37; Tom & Pat Leeson: 10-11, 20, 24, 31, 34-35, 38, 40, 43, 47, back cover; Stan Osolinski/Dembinsky Photo Associates: 13, 32; W. Perry Conway/Tom Stack & Associates: 18-19; John Shaw/Tom Stack & Associates: 26-27; Roy Toft/Tom Stack & Associates: 28-29.

NorthWord Press
5900 Green Oak Drive
Minnetonka, MN 55343
1-800-328-3895

Illustrations by John F. McGee / Book design by Russell S. Kuepper

National Wildlife Federation® is the nation's largest conservation, education and advocacy organization. Since 1936, NWF has educated people from all walks of life to protect nature, wildlife and the world we all share.

Ranger Rick® is an exciting magazine published monthly by National Wildlife Federation®, about wildlife, nature and the environment for kids ages 7 to 12. For more information about how to subscribe to this magazine, write: National Wildlife Federation, 8925 Leesburg Pike, Vienna, Virginia 22184.

NWF's World Wide Web Site www.nwf.org provides instant computer access to information about National Wildlife Federation, conservation issues and ideas for getting involved in protecting our world.

Library of Congress Cataloging-in-Publication Data
Fredericks, Anthony D.
    Elephants for kids / by Anthony D. Fredericks.
      p. cm.--(Wildlife for kids series)
    Summary: Explains where elephants live, what they look like, what they eat, and how they behave.
      ISBN 1-55971-678-9 (softcover)
    1. Elephants--Juvenile literature.   [1. Elephants.]   I. Title.
    II. Series.
    QL737.P98F72   1999
    599.67--dc21   98-42056

Printed in Malaysia

Elephants for Kids

Elephants often travel through a river to keep cool.

by Anthony D. Fredericks
illustrated by John F. McGee

All photographs in this book are of African elephants unless noted.

My mother is always telling me that I have a good memory. I can remember what to buy at the grocery store. I can remember the batting averages of all the players on my favorite baseball team. And I can remember lots of things in school, especially in science, which is my favorite subject.

Sometimes my mother tells me that I have a memory like an elephant. I like that, because elephants are my favorite animals.

A group of elephants is called a herd.

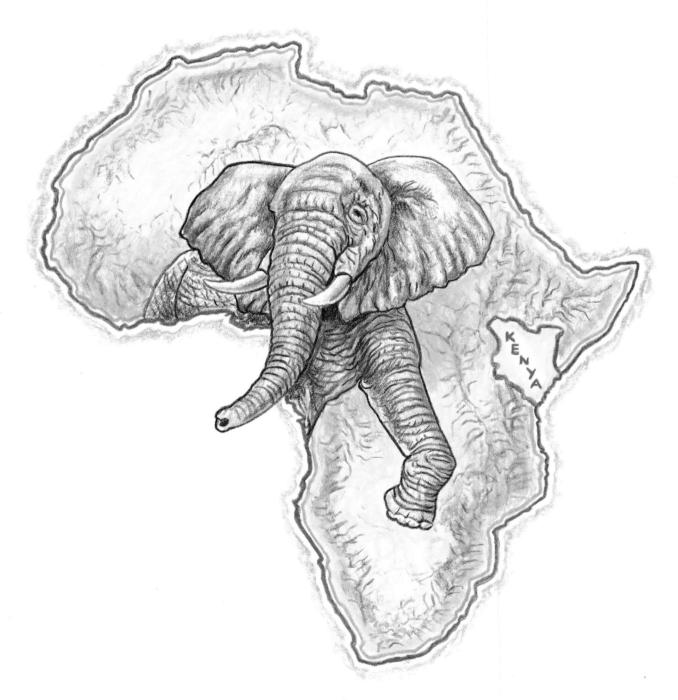

My name is Kwasi (KWAH-zee), and I'm 10 years old. My family moved to the United States from Kenya when I was very young. Kenya is a country in eastern Africa with large areas of grasslands, tall mountains, and lots of wild animals.

I don't remember a lot about my native country, but my father is always telling me about Kenya and its wild animals. I especially like his stories about elephants.

I've already learned a lot about elephants. For instance, a male is called a bull and a female is called a cow. A baby elephant is called a calf. Also, there are two different species (SPEE-sees), or kinds, of elephants: the African elephant and the Asian elephant.

The African elephant,
which lives in central
and southern Africa,
is the world's largest
land animal. A bull
elephant can weigh
up to 15,000 pounds.
That's about as heavy
as a school bus.
Cows are smaller.

A full-grown
African elephant
may stand 13 feet
high at the shoulder.
That's taller than a
basketball hoop.

African elephants have very large ears. Their ears can be 6 feet from top to bottom. And they seem to be shaped like their home continent of Africa. Also, African elephants have a single bump on the top of their head.

Pages 10-11: An elephant's hide, or skin, is very tough and its eyes are small.

9

The Asian elephant, which lives in India and several Southeast Asian countries, is smaller than its African relatives. An adult bull may weigh up to 12,000 pounds and stand about 10 feet tall.

Asian elephants have small ears. Some people say that their ears are shaped like the country of India. Asian elephants have two bumps on the top of their head.

An elephant's eyes are slightly larger than an adult human's eyes. Some people think that because an elephant's eyes are small for its size that it must have poor eyesight. But an elephant can see pretty well, even in the shaded forest. And it can see moving objects up to 150 feet away in bright sunlight.

The size and shape of the ears on this cow and calf
tell you they are Asian elephants.

Elephants walk at an average speed of about 5 miles per hour. Even though they are very large animals, they can run at speeds of about 35 miles per hour for short distances.

When elephants are moving quickly across dry savannas, they make a lot of dust.

Many people are surprised to learn that elephants walk on their tiptoes! The weight of an elephant rests on the tip of each toe and on thick pads behind the toes. Elephants are able to walk very quietly through the forest or across the savanna.

Elephants usually live together in two different types of herds. Adult bulls spend most of their time alone or with other bulls. Cows and calves live in their own herds, separate from the males except at mating time.

Cow and calf herds are always led by an older female, known as the matriarch (MAY-tree-ark). She is responsible for the safety of the herd and for helping them find water and food. Since the matriarch may live to be 60 or 70 years old, she may be the leader of a herd for many years.

This cow carefully watches over two calves.

Pages 18-19: Herds of cows and calves stay close as they travel across the hot savanna.

Elephants are very intelligent—and they really do have good memories. The matriarch is able to remember many migration paths, the location of watering holes, and where food can be found.

During the dry season, elephants may travel up to 30 miles in a day looking for food and water. Because she is older and has traveled more, the matriarch may have the best memory of all the elephants in a herd.

You can tell how deep this elephant went into the water by the wet line on its belly.

The first thing most people notice about an elephant is its trunk. An elephant's trunk is made of the nose, upper lip, and muscles of the elephant's face. In fact, an elephant's trunk has nearly 150,000 muscles, but no bones. It's one of the most amazing organs in the animal world.

Elephants sometimes greet each other by wrapping their trunks together. It's almost like a handshake! Elephants also use their trunks to draw up water for drinking or to spray over themselves in hot weather.

An adult elephant can suck up to 12 quarts of water into its trunk at one time and then squirt it into its mouth. During the dry season, elephants can put their trunks down their throats and take water out of their stomach. They spray this water over themselves to cool off.

Elephants use their trunks to wipe their eyes when something gets in them. They sometimes use them to wrestle. Trunks are also good "sniffers."

How would you like to be able to pick things up with your nose? That's what elephants do. They can use their trunks to pick up objects as small as a berry or a single blade of grass. An elephant's trunk can also lift heavy objects, such as logs weighing up to 600 pounds. That's like lifting me and seven of my friends all together!

African elephants have long trunks (up to 8 feet long), with two "fingers" at the tip. Asian elephants have shorter trunks with one triangular "finger." Using its trunk, an elephant can pick fruit, leaves, and branches from a tree up to a height of 20 feet. That's higher than a giraffe can reach!

Elephants must have good balance to be able to stretch for food like this.

Because elephants use their trunks to do so many things, it can take a calf 5 to 6 months to learn how to use its trunk. And when this "tool" gets tired, adult elephants often rest their trunks on the ends of their tusks.

An elephant's tusks are very long teeth, called incisors (in-SIZ-orz), that grow out from the upper jaw. They are made of ivory, which is similar to bone. Humans have incisors too, but they don't grow as long!

These young bulls are play-fighting with each other.

Both male and female African elephants have tusks. But most Asian females and many Asian males do not have tusks, or they are very short and not seen outside the jaw. (Scientists aren't sure why some elephants don't have tusks.) Tusks of both species continue to grow throughout an elephant's life at a rate of about 4 to 7 inches each year.

Many Asian elephants like this one have no tusks.

Elephants use their tusks for many things. They use them as tools to dig into the ground when looking for water. They use them as weapons—especially the males, which often fight with each other to protect their territories. Elephants also use their tusks as a sign of strength and superiority.

The world record weight for a single African elephant tusk is 259 pounds. The longest tusk on record measured 11 feet 6 inches. That's higher than the ceiling in my classroom at school!

When one elephant moves quickly toward another during a fight, it is called charging.

Just as people are right-handed or left-handed, elephants are right-tusked or left-tusked. If you look closely at an elephant's tusks you will notice that one of them is worn down more than the other. The one that shows the most wear is the one the elephant uses most of the time.

Another interesting thing about an elephant is its tail. An elephant's tail can be as long as 60 inches. The tail hairs on the end may be another 30 inches long. And the tips of the tail hairs often reach the ground.

An elephant's tail is used mostly to keep flies and other insects away. But it can also show an elephant's emotions, or feelings. When an elephant is frightened or angry it will hold its tail high in the air.

You can tell by the length of the tusks
that this is a right-tusked elephant.

An elephant uses its ears to help keep cool. In hot weather, an elephant flaps its ears to create a cooling breeze. This also cools the blood in the blood vessels in its ears. It's like built-in air conditioning!

Scientists who study animals are called zoologists (zoe-AH-luh-jists). Those who study elephants can identify individual elephants according to the blood vessel patterns in their ears. They are like "fingerprints." No two elephants have the same pattern.

This calf is learning to flap its ears to keep cool while eating.

Elephants also "talk" with their ears. The matriarch makes her ears stick out to signal members of the herd when there is danger nearby. She also moves her ears to tell them it's time to eat, rest, or travel.

Family members often greet one another by flapping their ears. When the whole herd becomes excited, they all flap their ears wildly. What a sight!

An elephant's skin is nearly hairless and very wrinkled.

My father's friend, Dr. Jacobson, has made several trips to the African country of Tanzania (tan-zan-EE-uh) to study how elephants communicate with each other. In her research, Dr. Jacobson learned that elephants use low-frequency sounds, called rumbling.

While humans are unable to hear these sounds, members of an elephant family can keep in touch with one another over distances of up to 6 miles.

Elephants communicate even while taking a mud bath.

They also make other noises that humans *can* hear.
Sometimes they raise their trunks high in the air
and make loud trumpeting sounds. These sounds,
which can be heard over long distances, usually
mean the elephant is angry or upset.

Elephants don't mind going into deep water to find the best food, like these river plants.

Because of their large size, full-grown elephants need to eat between 300 and 400 pounds of food every day. You and I, on the other hand, eat about 2 to 3 pounds of food a day. Eating that much food takes an elephant about 18 hours a day!

Most people eat lots of different kinds of food, like fruits, vegetables, breads, meat, and fish. Elephants, however, are herbivores (HERB-i-vorz). That means they eat only plant foods. Most of their diet is just plain grass. Sometimes they eat leaves and bark from trees. They also eat fruits, branches, and twigs.

In addition to all that food, an adult elephant can drink up to 3 gallons of water at one time or as much as 24 gallons of water in a day. Imagine if we drank that much water. That would be about 384 glasses of water every day!

Elephants also use water to keep cool. They give themselves lots of showers by spraying themselves with water using their trunks. The water cools them just as a shower cools us. Then, when the water on their skin evaporates, it cools them even more—just as evaporating sweat cools us. (Elephants do not have sweat glands in their skin as we do, so they must keep spraying themselves to keep from overheating.)

Elephants may wallow, or roll around, in a mud pit, which also keeps them cool. Elephants often seem to come in different colors, like red, brown, or black. But that's just the color of the mud they play in.

Elephants sometimes use their trunks to throw dust and mud over themselves. This forms a cooling and protective coating on their skins.

My parents sometimes complain about the wrinkles in their skin. But to an elephant, wrinkles are good. Wrinkles help elephants keep cool in hot weather. When an elephant takes a bath, the cracks and crevices in its skin trap moisture. This cooling moisture takes longer to evaporate from the elephant's skin. A wrinkly elephant keeps cooler much longer than one with fewer wrinkles.

This young cow's many wrinkles will help keep her cool after her bath.

But instead of telling my mother how helpful wrinkles can be, I decided to ask her about baby elephants. She told me that a female elephant usually has just 1 calf about every 4 years.

Gestation (jes-TA-shun) is the amount of time between when a male and female mate and the birth of the baby. For elephants, it is the longest in the animal world: 22 months. That means that a mother elephant is pregnant for almost 2 whole years.

A baby elephant weighs between 180 and 350 pounds when it is born. Newborn human babies weigh only about 7 to 10 pounds. Baby elephants grow very quickly. Very often they gain between 25 and 45 pounds in a month!

This tiny baby will begin to learn from many members of the herd.

45

Many females in the herd help teach and protect the growing calves. They are also very caring toward others in their herd. They may stay near a sick elephant for several days, watching over it and bringing it food.

Many people in countries around the world are working hard to protect elephants. Special game preserves and wild animal parks have been set up in some African and Asian countries.

When I grow up I would like to be a zoologist. I would like to visit my homeland of Kenya and help study and take care of the elephants!

Elephants spend a lot of time eating.

Other titles available in our popular

WILDLIFE *For Kids* SERIES™

Bats *For Kids*
• ISBN # 1-55971-545-6

Bears *For Kids*
• ISBN # 1-55971-134-5

Beavers *For Kids*
• ISBN # 1-55971-576-6

Bison *For Kids*
• ISBN # 1-55971-431-X

Butterflies *For Kids*
• ISBN # 1-55971-546-4

Cheetahs *For Kids*
• ISBN # 1-55971-665-7

Dolphins *For Kids*
• ISBN # 1-55971-460-3

Eagles *For Kids*
• ISBN # 1-55971-133-7

Foxes *For Kids*
• ISBN # 1-55971-637-1

Hawks *For Kids*
• ISBN # 1-55971-462-X

Kangaroos *For Kids*
• ISBN # 1-55971-595-2

Loon Magic *For Kids*
• ISBN # 1-55971-121-3

Manatees *For Kids*
• ISBN # 1-55971-539-1

Moose *For Kids*
• ISBN # 1-55971-211-2

Owls *For Kids*
• ISBN # 1-55971-475-1

Pandas *For Kids*
• ISBN # 1-55971-594-4

Raccoons *For Kids*
• ISBN # 1-55971-229-5

Sharks *For Kids*
• ISBN # 1-55971-476-X

Whales *For Kids*
• ISBN # 1-55971-125-6

Whitetails *For Kids*
• ISBN # 1-55971-122-1

Wild Horses *For Kids*
• ISBN # 1-55971-465-4

Wolves *For Kids*
• ISBN # 1-55971-123-X

See your nearest bookseller
or order by phone 1-800-328-3895

NORTHWORD
NORTHWORD PRESS